Under A

Blood Red

Moon

Poems by

Pamela Griffiths

PROFILE

I was born in Sheffield in September 1952;

Widow of Clive Griffiths. I have three children, a stepson and nine grandchildren.

I have a diploma in freelance journalism, a diploma in quality management and I'm retired from working for the NHS in Development and Quality management. I live in Loxley, Sheffield with my partner Sandy Hoffman.

I won the National Local Poem competition in 2011 with 'Home Sweet Home in Loxley Valley'. I've been published in over sixty poetry anthologies. My own poetry books include: 'Expressions of Life', 'Moments in Time', 'Life is a Spiral Staircase' and 'A Sheffield Lass'.

'The Stamp Master' is my first novel in the DCI Chrissie Charles detective thriller books and is now available in paperback and kindle format on Amazon. It has had some five star reviews' on Amazon I am currently working on the second Chrissie Charles book 'Heartless'.

For more information.

Please visit me on:

Website: www.pamelagriffiths.com

Twitter: @pamg56

Author fan page on Facebook – Author Pamela Griffiths

FOREWARD

Publishing the work of Pamela Griffiths is one of the main reasons why I got involved in the world of poetry.

I am a poet myself and I appreciate not just the upside of being a poet but also the very significant downside. Poetry is by nature, a lonely art.

But it is very important art – not just to the poet, but to the poet's audience. Poetry is certainly an 'Outlet' for a person's feelings, but what good is an outlet without someone to read, understand and feel the emotions, passions and thoughts expressed in each poem?

That's why poets like Pamela Griffiths need the help and support of United Press.

We're delighted to be able to provide a platform for the work of Pamela. This book is a unique record of Pamela's talents, visions and perceptions.

I hope you get the same pleasure in reading this book as we have had in putting it together and putting it before you, the reader.

Peter Quinn

A CIP catalogue record for this book is available from the British Library

ISBN – 978- 0-85781-641-2

CLASSIFICATION: POETRY

First published in Great Britain in 2016 by

United Press Ltd

Admail 3735

London

ECIB 1JB

Author's website: www.pamelagriffiths.com

CONTENTS

Following My Own Footsteps

I'm following my own footsteps
Retracing where they have been
Glancing at all the scenery
Over the great ravine

Tracing where my feet had trod
Along my walk of time
I can't believe how long it's been
Living this life of mine

The twists and turns were many
I had my own timeline
Following my own footsteps
I'm retracing this life of mine

All the people that I have met
Have influenced my dreams
As I follow my own footsteps
I've been here before it seems

I have walked along this way before
I have seen so many things
I really should go forward
To see what the future brings

As I follow the path I know so well
My footsteps disappear
I can't see any further ahead
Thoughts of the future I fear

Over hills and dales I go
Following along an old track
Sadness then overcomes me
As I meet myself coming back

When I was much younger
Way back in the day
My footsteps always faded
Then they were washed away

My life since then has evolved
I achieved so much back then
So I'm following in my own footsteps
To return to that life once again

In My Garden There Are Fairies

In my garden there are fairies, they are very real
Fairies I visit, I see, touch and feel
I have a place, where they gather and stay
They're always here for me, they never fly away
I visit them quite often, I look at them and smile
Drawn into my magical fairyland, I stay for a while
Some fairies have solar lamps, providing subdued light
My magical fairyland, can still be seen at night

I cherish the magical moments, I've been blessed with a lot
I consider myself very lucky, to have such a magical plot
Losing myself in the moments, as the fantasy takes a hold
It doesn't matter if it's scorching hot, or if it's freezing cold
In my Garden there are fairies, they stay with me
I will always love fairies, there for us all to see
They will never be frightened, or ever go away
The fairies in my garden, they are all here to stay

Lonely Lost Souls

Lonely lost souls are floating around
They cannot be heard, they don't make a sound
It's hard, it's a shame, they don't know why
Not truly believing, 'Did they really die?'

Looking around, where are they now?
Lost souls left to wander, not knowing why
As far as they know, life still goes on
Everything's changed now they have gone

Legacies left from the past have all changed
People buzz through life, as it's rearranged
Poor lonely lost souls, will be there forever
An umbilical cord keeps them there on a tether

Time is irrelevant, it doesn't last
What is our future is someone's past
Lonely lost souls trapped in time and space
Is this the finale of the human race?

Loving the dream

Loving the dream of falling in love
To find someone special that fits like a glove
To share a life with someone who cares
The answer to all my hopes and prayers
Love is profound a deep seated emotion
To find love there is no magic potion
Feeling the love and loving the dream
The love is there but cannot be seen

Love takes over there's no control
It invades the body and captures the soul
Loving the dream and overcoming fears
Finding true love after so many years
Words of love are spoken out loud
Either while alone or in a crowd
Laughing, loving, the emotional pleasure
Loving the dream a true love to treasure

Signs of amour are sent from above
Loving the dream and feeling the love
To give and share with a love so true
Is reciprocated right back at you
To share love provides a spiritual lift
A love of life is a wondrous gift
As each day passes I feel loved and serine
This is my life and I'm loving the dream

Profound Is My Love

So profound is my love
I feel the deep emotion
I know you love me too
A strong and true emotion

This love is so strong
Nothing can compare
We are very lucky
To have this love we share

Distinctive traits we hold
We are two souls merged as one
The love we share together
Has grown and never gone

Nothing can come between us
Together we are strong
A winding path in front of us
We follow, that's where we belong

Two hearts that beat in unison
Hearts full of wild desire
Passion and fury raged within
That set our hearts on fire

True love will never die
It will go on forever
We will stay in love
And we will always be together

Love can be so wonderful
Blessed are those who care
We are very happy
A profound love we share

Feelings are heightened
Thoughts are heightened too
I know you love me dearly
Just like I love you

Seasons of Love

Falling in love through the seasons
It doesn't matter at all
Whether it be in the winter
Or in autumn when the leaves fall

Love doesn't have any boundaries
It never fails to be
Love will go on forever
Throughout all eternity

Summer brings the sunshine
Enhancing love's sweet dreams
Spring brings hope for the future
A new beginning it seems

Each and every season
Has its own tale to tell
Colourful meanings surround them
We know all these seasons so well

All the seasons are lovely
Every one of them has its own theme
Sensual thoughts of love are born
Within a magical dream

The Festival of Love

It was in the summer solstice
Where our love first began
Druids gathered around us
In a gathering druid clan

The summer of love had arrived
Stonehenge was a magical place
I was in awe of the moment
I saw the look of love on your face

We wandered around the ancient stones
A deeper love could never be found
Cherishing every passionate moment
My heart was spinning around

The summer heat was scorching
It was very hard to breathe
True love had surrounded us
We didn't want to leave

The day seemed never ending
Magical moments we shared
The sun was almost setting
We talked, we loved, and we cared

As the sun went down on Stonehenge
We slowly moved away
The festival of love was now over
We will always remember this day

The Forest

I fell in love many years ago
For me it was love at first sight
I remember that magical moment
In the Forest in the moonlight

The trees were all around us
I stared into your dark brown eyes
You took my hand in your hand
My heart was captured by surprise

In the distance we could hear water
Flowing into a babbling brook
We followed the track towards it
Many hours that journey took

We could hear the foxes and nighthawks
As they hunted down their prey
We followed the stars in the moonlight
We had fallen in love that day

Walking along between the tall trees
Holding hands as we followed the track
Soon we found our campsite
In the darkness we found our way back

We went camping that week as strangers
But returned as a couple in love
The forest had enchanted us
A spell sent from heaven above

Many years we spent together
We were married and had children too
Lots of happy memories I had
Being in love with you

We returned to the enchanted forest
A special and wondrous place
That was such a long time ago
An era in time and space

Now I'm old and I'm looking back
I still remember that night
I'll never forget that moment
When I fell in love at first sight

Nothing can hold back the hands of time
We are all born to die
But if you have loved like I have
You are blessed and never ask why

The forest will always remind me
Of when I was young at heart
I will always remember
When love at first sight was the start

My true love was taken from me
He was ill and then he died
A part of me died with him
For years I grieved and cried

I can't believe he's no longer here
I still hear him in my mind
Sometimes I can feel him
In my soul he remains I find

I never grew old with my soul mate
That is such a shame
Memories of that forest back then
For eternity will remain

The World Is A Roundabout

The world is a roundabout
Spinning as we hop on
We turn with our world
But soon we will have gone

Others jump onto our world
They stay for a short spin
It's like a fairground ride
And the feelings are within

Joy and laughter can be good
But for some they fear the ride
There is nowhere they can run to
No place for them to hide

Others they just like the thrill
Adrenalin runs high
We all ride on this roundabout
Until the day we die

The roundabout is spinning
But we never get dizzy
We go about our business
We always seem so busy

The earth continues rotating
It will never stop
People they just come and go
Off and on they hop

A fairground ride of fun and fear
It's a perpetual emotional ride
What we gain on the swings
We will lose on the slide

Nothing lasts forever
That is very true
The world is just a roundabout
Governed by what we do

This Time

This time I'll make it count, life has a reason I'm sure
Looking back on many things, some things we can't ignore
This time I will try to do, the things I want to achieve
It's time to stop day dreaming, it's time to believe
I'll try not to be afraid, and overcome my fears,
Plenty of time to reflect, on my life over the years
I'll do things right this time, learn from my mistakes
Worrying doesn't help at all, I end up eating cakes
I'll calmly see, what I should have seen long ago
If only I was young again, knowing what I know
This time I realise, I'm human, nothing more.
I'll do what's right, never mind what's gone before
I'll be myself this time, not what others want me to be
I'll do the things I want to do, only answer to me,
I'll be alright this time, nothing will get in my way,
This time it's all my time, I'm going to live for today

Unrelenting Rain

The rain was falling in torrents,
With large and heavy drops
Soaking everything as it fell,
Dripping from all the rooftops
Pounding on the windows,
As the wind lashes the rain
The swirling blustery wetness
Is unrelenting again

Large thunderclouds overhead,
Drifted slowly away
The rain continued falling
It was set in for the day
A large screen of rain
Mars the view in the distance
The rain continues falling,
Meeting no resistance

Many people caught outside,
Run to escape the rain
This has happened many times
And it will happen again
These forces of nature
That no one can tame
No one can stop it,
This unrelenting rain

Under A Blood Red Moon

A fortune teller told me I'd meet a man soon

It would be romantic under a blood red moon

I didn't believe for a moment what she'd told me would be true

I've never seen a blood red moon there was nothing I could do

I'd forgotten what she'd told me I gave it no further thought

I went about my daily routine continued as I ought

I walked along one lonely night I was in my safe cocoon

I looked into the eerie sky to see a blood red moon

Looking at that blood red moon my inner thoughts had strayed

My darling you appeared to me I was shocked but I wasn't afraid

You're the ghost of my long lost past I lost you when you died

I have always loved you dearly many years I'd cried

I know love goes on forever the fortune teller was correct

Under a blood red moon that night your love I could never forget

Check out my website:

Author Pamela Griffiths